WORKBOOK

For

The Seven Principles for Making Marriage Work

A Guide to John Gottman's Book

By INSPIRED PRESS

INTRODUCTION

Marriage is a lifetime commitment that changes over time and tends to have a lot of issues as it progresses. While some couples adapt to change and move forward, others struggle to deal with and navigate these changes. With the help of this book, you will be able to discover some problems in your marriage and learn how to resolve them successfully. It includes seven concepts that were created from numerous tests throughout time. One of the benefits of the Seven Principles Approach is how well it can address relationships at all stages. This book is for single people who wishes to engage in short-term dating before making a long-term commitment. If you've already made a commitment and want to continue to cherish and protect what you have, it's also for you. The Seven Principles may assist you and your spouse maintain a healthy relationship if you are both going through significant changes or issues in your life.

CHAPTER 1: INSIDE THE SEATTLE LOVE LAB: THE TRUTH ABOUT HAPPY MARRIAGES

OBJECTIVES
1. The importance of emotional intelligence.
2. The effects of an unhappy marriage.
3. Letting go of marriage myths.

PREDICTING DIVORCE WITH A 91% ACCURACY
After years of research, the Love Lab can predict if a couple stays together after hearing them talk for 15 minutes. There are many people who believe they are marriage gurus. A responsible therapist advises couples based on their education, experience, intuition, family background, and maybe even religious conviction. However, it is not supported by concrete scientific data. Research by the Love Lab predicts divorce in a short time frame of marriage unlike older research. For instance, in a study of 130 newlywed couples, they identified 15 couples that would get divorced in 7 years based on analysis of their interactions. In reality, 17 couples got divorced, making the study's prediction rate 98% accurate. Although the study of long-term relationships has tremendously improved thanks to laboratory research's ability to predict divorce, that is not the main aim. The Seven Principles focuses on both divorce prediction and divorce prevention. The Love Lab's method of helping couples is founded on understanding what makes relationships successful rather than what causes them to fail. We no longer have to guess why some marriages stay happy; we can pinpoint what sets happy married couples apart from everyone else thanks to years of scientific data collection and analysis.

EMOTIONALLY INTELLIGENT MARRIAGES
Marriages can be made to work in different ways. Couples who are happily married are not more intelligent than others. However, they have discovered a dynamic in their regular interactions that keeps their negative emotions and ideas for one another from outweighing their favorable ones. They accept one another's demands rather than developing an atmosphere of hatred and disagreement. Instead of saying "Yes, but..." in response to a partner's request, they usually respond with "Yes, and..." This increases the sense of romance, play, joy, adventure, and learning in the marriage. This is an emotionally intelligent marriage. Spouses need to be emotionally intelligent; the likelihood that a couple will truly have a happily ever after increases with their emotional intelligence.

Couples can learn emotional intelligence; it can help prevent and solve a lot of issues.

WHY SAVE YOUR MARRIAGE?

Marriages end early because both partners do not appreciate the other's contributions until it is too late. Happy marriages tend to be taken for granted instead of being treated with the respect it requires. According to research by Lois Verbrugge and James House of the University of Michigan, an unhappy marriage can increase your risks of getting sick by around 35% and even reduce your life by an average of 4-8 years. While those who are happily married lead longer, healthier lives and scientists do not know why. People in unhappy marriages tend experience both physical and mental exhaustion. This causes further physical and mental wear and tear, which can manifest as different physical conditions and psychological issues. However, happily married couples tend to be healthier than most people. There is proof that a happy marriage can help you stay healthy by directly boosting your immune system. There was a huge difference between the immune-system reactions of the 50 couples who spent the night in the Love Lab. They specifically tested the response of some of each individual's white blood cells using blood samples from each subject. Results showed that happily married men and women generally showed a larger multiplication of these white blood cells when exposed to foreign invaders. Children also suffer when a marriage fails; it's not just the husband and wife. Research shows children who grew up in families with significant marital conflict often have increased levels of stress hormones. They experience higher rates of absenteeism, depression, behavioral issues, low academic success, and even school failure. Don't stay in a bad marriage for the sake of your children; raising them in a hostile environment is bad.

INNOVATIVE RESEARCH, REVOLUTIONARY FINDINGS

Marital satisfaction is important but there is barely any credible scientific study on how to maintain stable, happy marriages. Many studies on marital satisfaction rely on questionnaire responses from husbands and wives. This method is called the self-report method and it is not fully credible because people can lie in them. The Love Lab used more thorough techniques; they conducted 7 different studies that allowed them to follow the progress of 700 couples. They looked at different types of couples; newlyweds, couples with children, long-term couples etc. Most of their long-term research involved in-depth interviews with the partners, during which they discussed their marriage's history, relationship philosophies, and perspectives on other marriages. The heart rate, sweat output, breathing, and endocrine and immunological function of each couple were recorded and monitored. The tapes were played back to the couples and they were asked about what they were thinking and feeling. There were follow ups with the couples, at least once a year until the study ended, to see how their relationship was doing. Their data provided the first accurate look at the internal structure of marriage. These findings served as the foundation for the seven principles for successful marriage. When assessing the success of marriage counseling, the first year is a critical point. By that time, most couples who will relapse after counseling have already done so.

WHY MOST MARRIAGE THERAPY FAILS

You've probably received a lot of advice on your relationship especially if your relationship has or is having problems but not all advices are true or helpful. The largest misconception of all is that communication, and learning to overcome problems, is the key to love and a long-lasting, blissful marriage. Most couples prepare for battle when they find themselves in an argument and the avenues of communication may get blocked or shut down entirely as they become so preoccupied with how hurt they feel and proving their partner is incorrect. So it makes sense that couples would come up with answers if they quietly listened to each other's viewpoints and it does help to develop and preserve relationships. However, this method is thought to be all that a couple needs to succeed and that is not true. Another advice is active listening which is the most popular technique for conflict resolution. Couples are expected to solve their problems without hostility, forcing them to examine their differences from each other's perspective and regardless of the problem, this is another strategy that is frequently advised. Conflict resolution is promoted as a cure for unhappy marriages and a way to keep healthy marriage strong. The founders of marital therapy modified it from methods used in individual psychotherapy by renowned psychotherapist Carl Rogers. His approach entails responding in a nonjudgmental and accepting manner to all feelings and thoughts the patient expresses. The goal is to create an empathetic environment for the patient to feel comfortable disclosing their innermost feelings and ideas to the therapist. It makes sense to teach couples this kind of unconditional understanding because marriage is a relationship where people should feel safe being themselves. However, active listening and conflict resolution alone are not enough for therapy to work.

Kurt Hahlweg and his colleagues conducted a marital therapy study in Munich and discovered that typical couples were still in distress even after using active-listening techniques. Only a few couples experienced success, and they all reverted within a year. This doesn't mean active listening is invalid; it can still be used to settle issues. However, marriage cannot be saved by using just these tactics; all 7 principles are necessary. Therapy fails because good conflict resolution does not lead to successful marriages.

EXPLODING MORE MYTHS ABOUT MARRIAGE

The most common myth regarding good marriages is that you can save your relationship by just learning how to speak more sensitively. There are lots of other myths and some are:

1. Common interests keep you together: How you engage while pursuing those interests will determine everything.
2. You scratch my back and .: According to experts, the difference between healthy relationships and toxic ones is the fact that in healthy relationships, partners return each other's kind words and actions. The couple works under the unspoken agreement that they will pay back any kind words or deeds. This agreement has failed in unhappy relationships, leaving behind resentment and anger. However, keeping track of who has done what and when for whom in a marriage is actually a sign of instability. Your marriage might have problems if you find yourself keeping score with your spouse over a particular issue.
3. Avoiding conflict will ruin your marriage: Many happy, long-lasting relationships continue despite avoiding conflict. Couples have different conflict styles; some people argue frequently, some want to avoid conflicts at all costs, and some are able to speak out their differences and come to an agreement without ever raising their voices. As long as the style suits both persons, there is no style that is better than the other.
4. Men are not biologically built for marriage: According to this belief, men are inherently polygamous and are therefore not good candidates for monogamy. The likelihood of extramarital affairs is, however, more influenced by opportunities than by gender. The number of extramarital affairs among women has increased dramatically since more women now work outside the home.
5. Men and women are from different planets: Numerous best-selling books claim that the reason why men and women can't get along is that men are from Mars while women are from Venus. However, happily married heterosexual couples are also "aliens" to one another. Gender differences do not necessarily result in marital issues.

We all understand that maintaining a long-lasting relationship requires courage, tenacity, and resilience. However, once you realize what really makes a marriage work, saving or protecting your own will be easier.

LESSONS

1. Being emotional intelligent helps to prevent and solve a lot of issues in a relationship.
2. Unhappy marriages can increase your risks of getting sick and reduce your life.
3. You should feel safe being yourself in your relationships.
4. Unhappy marriages don't just affect the couple involved, it can also affect children and cause them stress.
5. Good conflict resolution does not lead to successful marriages.
6. Maintaining a long-lasting relationship requires courage, tenacity, and resilience.

QUESTIONS

1. What are the characteristics of an emotionally intelligent marriage?

_____
_____
_____
_____
_____
_____
_____
_____
_____
_____
_____
_____
_____

2. What kind of marriage do you currently have with your spouse?

_____
_____
_____
_____
_____
_____
_____
_____

3. Why is emotional intelligence important in a relationship?

_____
_____
_____
_____
_____
_____
_____
_____
_____
_____
_____
_____
_____

4. What are the benefits of a happy marriage?

_____
_____
_____
_____
_____
_____
_____
_____
_____
_____

5. How has been in an unhappy relationship affected you?

_____
_____
_____
_____

6. What kind of advice have you given and received about relationships?

_____
_____
_____
_____
_____
_____
_____
_____
_____
_____

7. How did your parents' marriage affect you as a child?

_____
_____
_____
_____
_____
_____
_____
_____
_____
_____

8. What myths have you heard about marriage?

_____
_____

_____

_____

_____

_____

_____

_____

_____

_____

9. How has therapy helped your marriage?

_____

_____

_____

_____

_____

_____

_____

_____

_____

_____

10. What conflict style exists in your relationship?

_____

_____

_____

_____

_____

_____

_____

_____

_____

_____

_____

_____

_____

CHAPTER 2: WHAT DOES MAKE MARRIAGE WORK?

OBJECTIVES
1. Understanding the concept of positive sentiment override.
2. Building your friendship.
3. Identifying repair attempts.

The sad reality is that encouraging couples to fight more nicely isn't enough to breathe new life into their marriages. There is no such thing as the ideal union. Despite the fact that many couples claim to be incredibly happy together, they constantly argued because of the stark differences in their personalities, interests, and family beliefs. Like the miserable couples, they quarreled over various things. It is a surprise they were able to overcome these obstacles and keep long-lasting, fulfilling relationships. Although no two marriages are alike, successful marriages have seven things in common. Even if they are unaware of it, all happily married couples adhere to the Seven Principles.

FRIENDSHIP VERSUS FIGHTING

The fundamental principle of the Seven Principles method is the knowledge that successful marriages are built on strong friendships. Couples in successful marriages often have a close relationship and know each other extremely well. They have a deep respect for one another and show it through acts of kindness. Friendship is the strongest defense against negative feelings toward your spouse; it feeds the flames of romance. Robert Weiss, a psychologist at the University of Oregon, is the inventor of the psychological concept known as "positive sentiment override," or PSO. It is when married couples maintain their friendship even though they have arguments and issues. Their positive impressions of one another and their marriage is higher than the negative ones. Losing the equilibrium as a couple would require a very intense disagreement. They have positive views of their relationship and positive goals for their future as a couple. They have a history of being tolerant of one another. If your connection begins to deteriorate significantly, it will be harder to repair. Most relationships start off with such a strong foundation that it can be challenging for either partner to notice things deteriorating. However, this happy condition is short-lived. The friendship begins to seem abstract as anger, rage, and frustration grow over time. Finally, everything is viewed negatively as they reach a sentiment override. Words are taken personally, even when spoken in a neutral tone.

BUILDING YOUR SOUND RELATIONSHIP HOUSE

Happy couples feel good because they both have a basic understanding of one another's emotional needs. This is called Attunement. Partners grow more skilled in it, which strengthens their bond and makes their future more stable and bright. Attunement comes naturally to some couples but for other, it requires more effort. Partners build their Sound Relationship House as they get to know and connect with one another. The different floors or levels of the Sound Relationship House are made up of the Seven Principles. The seven principles are closely related to trust and commitment which protect their relationship house. Using the principles of game theory, The Love Lab developed formulas that can determine if partners have a high level of trust or are likely to experience infidelity in the future. When a couple constantly assumes the worst about one another, they end up imprisoned in the Roach Motel, a common situation of negativity. Constant strife and bad feelings are characteristics of this horrible place. Couples "check in" to it before realizing they can't leave. Couples who end up stranded in the Roach Motel assume that their partner is naturally selfish. As the relationship degenerates into a zero-sum game, one partner's achievement is seen as the other's failure. Because of mistrust, the sense of security is lost. Even though we equate infidelity with sexual relations, having a sexual relationship outside of marriage is just one type of betrayal that can put a couple in danger once their Sound Relationship House has been destroyed. A betrayal is any behavior that prioritizes the partner over all else. Other types of betrayals can also ruin relationships. Some examples are being emotionally aloof, supporting a parent against your spouse, showing disrespect for the other person etc. The truth is most of us occasionally act faithless but the real danger is when either partner regularly underperforms in the marriage. According to the Love Lab study, betrayal is the root cause of all strained relationships. Most couples are neither stuck in mistrust nor completely skilled at living together. Most long-term relationships fall somewhere between these two extremes. This shows that even in dysfunctional relationships, love can flourish. The key is to value friendship and grow in your sensitivity to one another. Although you may still disagree, arguments won't be as damaging.

REPAIRS: A HAPPY COUPLE'S SECRET WEAPON

Rediscovering or rekindling friendship gives couples a secret weapon that ensures their arguments don't escalate, but it doesn't stop them from fighting. Repair attempts are any words or deeds that stop negativity from becoming out of control. A couple that is close naturally becomes skilled at offering one another repair attempts and at correctly interpreting those that are sent their way. However, when couples are in negative override, even simple repair attempts may have a low success rate. A key determinant of the success of a couple's marriage is the outcome of their repair attempts. The strength of their marriage friendship is what decides the outcome of their repair attempts. It takes more than being kind to improve your marriage friendship. Even if you believe your friendship is already strong, you might be surprised to learn there is still room for growth.

THE PURPOSE OF MARRIAGE

Husband and wife have a strong sense of meaning in the best marriages. They don't just get along; they also encourage one another's goals and objectives and provide their shared life a sense of direction. Failure to accomplish this in a marriage is usually what leads to husband and wife getting into pointless arguments or feeling alone and isolated in their union. Most marital issues cannot be settled and couples need to realize that. This is because most of their conflicts are due to significant lifestyle, personality, or moral differences. Couples must recognize the fundamental differences fueling their conflict and learn to live with it through mutual honor and respect. Only then can they fill their marriage with a sense of shared meaning and purpose. No matter how your relationship is currently doing, applying the seven principles of marriage can lead to significant improvement. Understanding what happens when the Seven Principles are not followed is the first step toward improving your marriage. Learning from the mistakes can also help your marriage.

LESSONS

1. No two marriages are the same but successful marriages follow the Seven Principles.
2. Infidelity is not the only form of betrayal in relationships; others include being aloof, being disrespectful etc.
3. Repair attempts are any words or deeds that stop negativity from becoming out of control.
4. There is always room for growth in your friendship with your partner.
5. It is impossible to solve all your marriage issues.
6. It is important that you learn from the mistakes you make in your relationships and not repeat them.

QUESTIONS

1. How often do you and your spouse fight and disagree?

_____
_____
_____
_____
_____
_____
_____
_____
_____
_____
_____
_____

2. What differences do you and your partner tend to fight about?

_____
_____
_____
_____
_____
_____
_____
_____
_____
_____

3. How close are you with your spouse?

_____
_____
_____
_____
_____
_____
_____

4. What are the characteristics of the Roach Motel?

_____
_____
_____
_____
_____
_____
_____
_____
_____
_____
_____

5. What forms of betrayal have you experienced in relationships?

_____
_____
_____
_____
_____
_____
_____
_____
_____
_____
_____
_____
_____
_____
_____

6. What are your repair attempts?

_____
_____

_____
_____
_____
_____
_____
_____
_____
_____

7. What's the difference between a positive and negative override?

_____
_____
_____
_____
_____
_____
_____
_____
_____
_____

8. What mistake is a learning experience in your marriage?

_____
_____
_____
_____
_____
_____
_____
_____
_____
_____

9. What are the current goals in your relationship?

_____
_____

10. How is your relationship different from that of others?

CHAPTER 3: HOW I PREDICT DIVORCE

OBJECTIVES
1. Identifying the four horsemen.
2. How men and women are different.
3. Knowing when the end is near.

THE FIRST SIGN: HARSH START-UP
A discussion has a harsh start-up when it begins with criticism and/or sarcasm. According to the research, even if there are numerous attempts to "make nice" in between, your talk will unavoidably conclude on a negative note if it starts out harshly. The first three minutes of a conversation allows you to predict how it will turn out. So, it's best to cut a conversation short, take a break, then start it again if it gets off to a rough start.

THE SECOND SIGN: THE FOUR HORSEMEN
There are certain negative emotions called the Four Horsemen of the Apocalypse; they can destroy a relationship if they are not controlled. They are:
1. Criticism: You'll always have complaints about the person you live with. However, there is a difference between criticism and complaint. A complaint focuses on a certain act or occurrence. It is made up of 3 components: how you feel, a certain circumstance, what you prefer, need, and want. A criticism is general and an unfavorable opinion or conclusion about the character or personality of the other person. Complaints are gentle start-ups while criticisms are harsh start-ups. "You always" and "you never" statements are two common forms of criticism. However, you can transform any complaint into a criticism just by saying "What is wrong with you?" Relationships often involve criticism and a bit of it doesn't lead to divorce. However, the issue with criticism is that it opens the door for the other, deadlier horsemen when it happens often.
2. Contempt: Feeling superiority toward one's partner leads to contempt. It is a disrespectful act. Two forms of contempt are sarcasm and cynicism. Name-calling, eye-rolling, ridicule, and aggressive humor are also other forms of contempt. Contempt leads to more issues. Belligerence, the relative of contempt, also destroys relationships. It is a manifestation of violent anger that involves threat or provocation.
3. Defensiveness: Being defensive is a partner-blaming strategy. You're basically saying, "The issue is with you, not with me." The "innocent victim"

strategy is a common form of defensiveness; it basically says, "Why are you picking on me?" Defensiveness in any form makes conflict worse.

4. Stonewalling: When conflicts in marriages get off to a bad start, there are insults, then defensiveness, and eventually one partner tunes out. This is called Stonewalling. Stonewalling is a behavior that both husbands and women engage in, but research shows that men do it more. During a typical conversation, the listener will give many cues to the speaker to show that he is paying attention. A stonewaller typically keeps quiet and just turns his head. The stonewaller acts as if he couldn't care less if he even hears what you're saying. Stonewalling typically enters a marriage later than the other three horsemen. This is why newlywed men are less likely to experience it. It takes time for the first three horsemen's negativity to build up to a point where stonewalling is an acceptable exit.

THE THIRD SIGN: FLOODING

Flooding is a feeling of being psychologically and physically overpowered. It happens when your spouse's criticism comes at you abruptly and violently, leaving you in shock. Since you feel so helpless, you learn to do anything to stop a replay. When your partner criticizes or rejects you more regularly, you become hyper-vigilant for clues that they might "blow" again.

THE FOURTH SIGN: BODY LANGUAGE

When you examine couples for physical changes during a tense argument, you can see how physically upsetting flooding is. An example is an increased heart rate. The "fight or flight response" is brought on by hormonal changes, including the release of adrenaline. The extent of these modifications makes it simple to assume that, if the couple's dynamic doesn't change, they will get divorced, especially if one partner usually dominates marriage-related conversations. There are two reasons why frequent flooding promotes divorce. First of all, they show that one spouse has excruciating emotional agony when speaking to the other spouse. Second, the physical signs of feeling overburdened make it very hand to engage in meaningful discussion. When your body goes into overdrive during a quarrel, your body is reacting to a very fundamental warning mechanism that we inherited from our ancestors. All those uncomfortable signs, such as sweating and a beating heart, are caused by your body's perception that your current situation is unsafe.

MEN AND WOMEN REALLY ARE DIFFERENT

The stonewaller in 85% of heterosexual relationships is the husband. This is mostly due to our evolutionary history. While the males excelled at cooperative hunting and protection, the females specialized in raising young. Your level of relaxation as a nursing mother affects how much milk you produce. Natural selection would therefore favor a female who could quickly calm herself down after being anxious. Her ability to maintain her composure might increase her children's chances of surviving by maximizing the nutrition they received. Natural selection, however, would favor the opposing response in males. Being attentive was a vital survival trait for early hunters. Therefore, if their adrenaline was produced quickly and they did not cool down as easily, males were more likely to survive and reproduce. This gender difference also has an impact on the things that both men and women frequently think about when facing marital stress. In a test done by the Love Lab, they invited couples to view their arguments on video and then describe their thoughts as soon as our sensors noticed they were overwhelmed. According to their responses, men are more inclined to think negative thoughts that keep them in discomfort, while women are more likely to think calming thoughts that encourage them to calm down and be accommodating. Obviously, these rules don't apply to all men and all women. However, similar gender differences in the body's physiological and psychological reactions to stress are observed in most heterosexual partnerships. Due to these differences, the wife brings up delicate subjects in most relationships because she is biologically better able to handle the stress while the husband will want to steer clear of the subject. He could get aggressive and build a wall. However, marriage doesn't necessarily end in divorce if this happens frequently. There is a problem when the four horsemen settle down permanently. Experiencing chronic stress leads to emotional detachment, which breeds loneliness. Without help, the couple either divorces or continues to live in the same home but with different lives.

THE FIFTH SIGN: FAILED REPAIR

The four horsemen and the flooding that follows them take time to overwhelm a marriage. However, a single chat between newlyweds can be used to predict divorce. How is this possible? By looking at every argument a couple has, you can get a sense of their pattern, which hardly changes until they get the correct kind of support. Whether a couple's repair fails or succeeds is an important part of their pattern. Marriages are preserved through repair efforts. When the four horsemen rule a couple's communication, repair attempts aren't appreciated. When you're stressed out, you can't hear a spoken word of peace. In unhappy marriages, the four horsemen and failed attempts at rehabilitation create a feedback loop. The more dismissive and defensive the couple is with one another, the more flooding occurs and the more difficult it is to hear and respond to a repair. The disrespect and defensiveness only grow as a result of the unheard repair, this increases flooding and makes it more difficult to hear the repair attempt until one partner eventually leaves. Failed repair attempts are a sign of an unhappy future. When the four horsemen appear but the couple's attempts at mending are successful, the outcome is typically a happy marriage. There are various successful repair attempts in emotionally intelligent marriages. Everybody has a different strategy. The main thing that affects whether a repair is successful or unsuccessful is the status of the marriage. Ironically, there are more repair attempts in unhappy marriages than in happy ones. The unhappy couples keep trying, even when their attempts to heal things keep failing.

THE SIXTH SIGN: BAD MEMORIES

When negativity takes over a relationship, the couple's current, future and past lives as a couple are in danger. When asked about their marriage's history, people who have a negative opinion of their spouse and their union tend to exaggerate the facts. You can predict a couple's likelihood of divorcing based on their responses to questions about their early courtship, wedding, and first year of marriage, even if you are not aware of their current feelings. Most couples have high expectations when they get married. In a happy marriage, spouses tend to remember their early years with nostalgia. Even if things weren't perfect, they tend to remember more positive parts and feelings. But when a marriage fails, the opposite happens. Another troubling sign is when one or both spouses have trouble remembering the past.

THE END DRAWS NEAR

Without the right help, a couple's marriage will collapse if they have rewritten their history and their bodies and brains make it difficult for them to communicate and resolve their current problems. Due to the constant expectation of conflict, such couples are in a state of high alert at all times, which strains their relationships. The logical conclusion is that they end the relationship. In this stage of their marriage, a couple could occasionally go to counseling. They don't always act disrespectfully, or stonewall, so it could look like nothing is wrong on the surface. A novice therapist can believe that their issues don't go very far. But in reality, one or both of them already stopped caring about the marriage emotionally. Laboratory research shows that these emotionally detached couples eventually get divorced, but it takes them an average of 16 years instead of 5.6

years for couples whose conversations are dominated by the four horsemen. Divorce is one way that some people leave a marriage. Others accomplish this by being a unit but living separate lives. There are four last stages, regardless of the path, that signal the end of a relationship.

1. The couple considers their marital issues to be serious.
2. It seems pointless to discuss issues. Partners make independent efforts to find solutions.
3. The couples live independent lives.
4. The onset of loneliness.

When a couple reaches the final stage, one or both partners may have an affair. However, this betrayal is a sign and not the root of a failing marriage. Couples usually wait until their marriage is already in crisis before they start looking for help. If they knew what to look for, the warning flags were nearly always present early on. The warning signs are:

1. what couples actually say to one another
2. the failure of their attempts at mending
3. physiological responses
4. Persistent unhappy thoughts about their union.

BUT IT'S NOT OVER TILL IT'S OVER

With the correct intervention, even a marriage that is close to collapse can be saved. Sadly, the majority of marriages at this stage get the wrong kind of help. The couple will be bombarded by therapists with suggestions for resolving their conflicts and enhancing their communication. The key to reviving a relationship is not how you handle your disagreements but how you engage with each other when you're not fighting. Your friendship with each other fosters the romance, passion, and fantastic sex. Therefore, no matter where your marriage is at the moment, it will benefit if you encourage, rekindle, or, if required, revive your friendship. Examining how much you actually know about one another is the first step.

LESSONS

1. A harsh start-up is when a conversation starts with criticism or sarcasm.
2. Belligerence is a manifestation of violent anger that involves threat or provocation.
3. In most relationships, men are the stonewallers.
4. The status of a marriage is what determines if a repair attempt is successful or not.

5. Betrayal is a sign and not usually the cause of the end of a relationship or marriage.
6. The four horsemen that cause issues in relationships are criticism, contempt, defensiveness and stonewalling.
7. Every relationship can be saved with the right kind of help.
8. Building a friendship in your relationship fosters romance and passion.

QUESTIONS

1. What's the difference between complaint and criticism?

_____
_____
_____
_____
_____
_____
_____
_____
_____
_____
_____

2. Which of the four horsemen do you mostly experience in your marriage?

_____
_____
_____
_____
_____
_____
_____
_____
_____
_____

3. What are the different forms of contempt?

_____
_____
_____

_____
_____
_____
_____
_____
_____
_____
_____

4. What are the effects of failed repair attempts?

_____
_____
_____
_____
_____
_____
_____
_____
_____
_____
_____

5. What expectations did you have about marriage and how have they changed recently?

_____
_____
_____
_____
_____
_____
_____
_____
_____
_____
_____

6. When was the last time you experienced flooding?

_____
_____
_____

_____
_____
_____
_____
_____
_____
_____
_____
_____

7. How do you know a relationship is ending?

_____
_____
_____
_____
_____
_____
_____
_____
_____
_____

8. How is your friendship with your partner?

_____
_____
_____
_____
_____
_____
_____
_____
_____
_____

9. When did you know it was time to leave your last relationship?

_____
_____
_____

10. How much does your partner know about you and how much do you know about them?

CHAPTER 4: PRINCIPLE 1: ENHANCE YOUR LOVE MAPS

OBJECTIVES
1. Enhancing your love map.
2. The importance of knowledge.

Many married couples ignore the specifics of their partner's existence. They don't fully understand the other's joys, likes, dislikes, concerns, or stresses. However, emotionally intelligent couples are very familiar with one another. A love map is the area of your brain where you keep all the relevant details about your partner's life. Couples need to keep their knowledge current as the facts and emotions in their spouse's world change, remembering the key moments in each other's history. You can't genuinely know your partner if you don't have a love map like that. How can you truly love someone if you don't know them well?

IN KNOWLEDGE THERE IS STRENGTH
Knowledge is the source of not just love but also the strength to endure marital difficulties. Couples that have detailed love maps of one another's worlds are considerably better able to deal with challenging circumstances and conflict. One of the primary causes of marital misery and divorce is having children. Love maps help to protect marriages after huge changes. This is because the husband and wife were already in the habit of staying current and were aware of what each other was feeling and thinking. But when lives change so abruptly, it's possible for a marriage to lose its direction if couples don't start off with a strong understanding of one another. A significant change can cause a couple to go off course if they don't have a clear love map. Getting to know each other shouldn't feel like a burden.

THE NEXT STEP
Getting to know your partner better and opening up to them on a deeper level takes time. It is a continuous process. Look forward to updating your knowledge of one another and yourself. Prepare some questions for your partner. Despite their strength, love maps are just the beginning. Couples that are successfully married don't "simply" know each other. They use their love maps to communicate their understanding, affection and admiration for one another.

LESSONS
1. A love map is the area of your brain where you keep all the relevant details about your partner's life.

2. You cannot truly love your partner if you don't know them well.
3. Love maps protect marriages after a huge change.
4. Getting to know your partner is a continuous process; you can't know everything because people change over time.

QUESTIONS

1. What specifics do you know about your partner's interests or recent occurrences in their lives?

_____

_____

_____

_____

_____

_____

_____

_____

_____

_____

2. How did having a child affect your marriage?

_____

_____

_____

_____

_____

_____

_____

_____

_____

3. What's the importance of a detailed love map?

_____

_____

_____

_____

_____
_____
_____
_____
_____
_____
_____
_____

4. What has changed about your partner recently?

_____
_____
_____
_____
_____
_____
_____
_____
_____
_____
_____

5. How would you say you have changed recently?

_____
_____
_____
_____
_____
_____
_____
_____
_____

6. What improvements need to be made to the current love map in your relationship?

_____

_____

_____

_____

_____

_____

_____

_____

_____

_____

_____

_____

_____

_____

_____

_____

_____

_____

_____

_____

7. What significant changes have affected your relationship?

_____

_____

_____

_____

_____

_____

_____

_____

_____

_____

_____

_____

_____

CHAPTER 5: PRINCIPLE 2: NURTURE YOUR FONDNESS AND ADMIRATION

OBJECTIVES
1. Building fondness and admiration.
2. Learning to cherish your partner.

A couple's fond memories of their early years served as proof that, despite their issues, there's still traces of a fondness and admiration system. This shows that they believe that the other person deserved of admiration and respect. If there is still a system of affection and admiration between couples, their marriage can be saved. Fondness and appreciation are the key ingredients of a successful and long-lasting relationship. Without it, the relationship cannot be repaired.

LEARNING FROM HISTORY
How a couple sees their past is a good indicator of their fondness and admiration system is still in place. Asking a couple about their current problem might lead t them talking negatively. But if you ask them about the past, you can sense some good emotions if there is a fondness and admiration system. In some marriages, hostility has spread, removing any happy memories. They remember very little about the beginning of their relationship. Having a positive view of your partner and your marriage is a terrific buffer during difficult times.

THE ANTIDOTE TO CONTEMPT
Happily married people get along with one another. A good marriage can be preserved by reminding yourself of your partner's good qualities. Basically, affection and admiration are cures for contempt. When you disagree with your partner, you are less likely to act disgusted with them if you continue to respect them. Love and admiration keep you from falling into any of the four horsemen. Your marriage is in jeopardy if your affection and admiration are completely gone. The secret to reviving fondness and admiration is to look for qualities in the other person you can admire. Tell your partner what you've noticed and are thankful for; they don't have to be big things. According to Elizabeth Robinson and Gail Price, unhappy couples only notice half of the positive interactions that happen with their spouse. They failed to notice 50% of their partner's positive behaviors because they're used to focusing on their partner's errors. Contempt is a destructive agent that weakens the union between a husband and wife. When you're more in touch with your loving feelings for one another, you're less likely to treat your partner with disrespect during conflict.

FANNING THE FLAMES

Reviving or strengthening your fondness and admiration is not difficult. You can revive buried emotions by reflecting on and discussing them. This can be done by taking some time to reflect on your relationship and what makes them special to you. When you sincerely show your gratitude for your partner and your marriage, your bond becomes stronger.

LEARNING TO CHERISH YOUR PARTNER

What thoughts do you have about your partner when you're not together? Cherishing is an important part of a couple's affection and admiration system. It happens when you increase your positive thoughts about your partner and reduce the negative ones when you're apart. By actively focusing on your partner's good qualities, you can cultivate gratitude for what you have rather than resentment for what you don't have. Many couples don't know they are not cherishing each other.

LESSONS

1. Fondness and appreciation are the key ingredients of a successful and long-lasting relationship.
2. Remembering your partner's good qualities can help preserve a marriage.
3. The secret to reviving fondness and admiration is to look for qualities in the other person you can admire.
4. Cherishing happens when you increase your positive thoughts about your partner and reduce the negative ones when you're apart.
5. You can revive buried emotions by reflecting on and discussing them.

QUESTIONS

1. What do you remember about the early days with your partner?

_____

_____

_____

_____

_____

_____

_____

_____

_____

_____

_____

2. What level of fondness and admiration do you currently have for your spouse?

_____

_____

_____

_____

_____

_____

_____

_____

_____

_____

3. What are the benefits of a fondness and admiration system?

_____

_____

_____

_____

_____

_____

_____

_____

_____

_____

4. What are your partner's good qualities?

_____

_____

_____

_____

_____

_____

_____

_____
_____
_____

5. What makes your relationship special to you?

_____
_____
_____
_____
_____
_____
_____
_____
_____
_____
_____
_____

6. How do you feel about your partner when you're apart?

_____
_____
_____
_____
_____
_____
_____
_____
_____

7. How can you revive your fondness and admiration for your partner?

_____
_____
_____
_____

8. At what point did you lose respect for your partner?

CHAPTER 6: PRINCIPLE 3: TURN TOWARD EACH OTHER INSTEAD OF AWAY

OBJECTIVES
1. Coping with your partner's negative emotions.
2. Using active listening.

Couples that frequently have boring basic conversations are likely to stay happy. They are actually interacting during these conversations and this builds mutual trust. Those who don't are probably going to get lost. Our perception of romance has been spoilt by Hollywood. In real life, every time you let your spouse know they are cherished, you maintain your relationship. In a marriage, partners constantly compete with one another and bid for each other's love, devotion, humor, or support. Each bid is met by the partner turning either toward or away from the spouse. The foundation of trust, emotional connection, passion, and a fulfilling sex life is a tendency to turn toward your spouse. Bids play an important role in relationships. In the Love Lab's six-year follow-up of newlyweds, they discovered that couples who remained married accepted their partner's bids 86% of the time, but those who ended up getting divorced had done so only 33% of the time on average. Basically, most of disputes between couples in both groups came from those unsuccessful attempts to connect rather than specific issues. There is a reason why minor incidents determine the success of a relationship. Every time a couple turns toward one another, they make a deposit into their emotional bank account. They are saving in case of a severe life crisis or conflict. Such couples have a lot of goodwill stored up, so they are less likely to waver into mistrust and negativity during tough times. The first step in turning toward one another more is realizing how important these simple moments are to your marriage. Remind yourself that if you are supportive of one another, your marriage will be lot stronger and more passionate. Many people think that taking a trip will make it easier for them to reconnect with their partner. But a romantic outing only makes things better if the couple has kept the flame alive by staying in touch in little ways. One benefit of turning toward one another is how simple it is to do. A single modest action can spark a chain of subsequent ones. Just get started, and things will improve by themselves.

TWO OBSTACLES TO TURNING TOWARD
Couples struggle to move toward one another and build trust due to two circumstances. You may prevent these stumbling blocks in your relationship by following these steps:

1. "Missing" a bid because it's wrapped in anger or other negative emotion: When a partner tries to connect, the spouse might not notice, especially if the marriage is struggling. This is because it often sounds negative. The partner then responds negatively and fails to see the hidden request. Before you react defensively to your partner's harsh words, pause for a moment and search for a bid. Instead of focusing on the delivery, pay attention to the bid. Take five slow, deep breaths if you find it difficult to resist the temptation to defend yourself. Work on softening your start-up if you habitually wrap criticism around bids.
2. Bring distracted by the wired world: Turning toward can also be hard due to the Internet and digital devices. There are benefits of the internet but there are also detriments. Because we can be contacted at all hours of the day and night, the close communication that build romantic love and family life may suffer. Constantly checking your emails, posts, tweets, and texts can become an addiction. When one partner is unavailable or has a hectic schedule, it can be a problem. Some couples unintentionally use technology as a form of self-distraction during conflict. A partner who is hesitant to communicate or who is prepared to stonewall can use it to avoid conversations. We rarely notice how addictive these technologies can be. The solution to this growing problem is for both partners to acknowledge that there is a problem between them and implement rules that work for both of them.

USING ACTIVE LISTENING DURING STRESS REDUCING CONVERSATIONS

1. Take turns: Each partner gets to complain for 15 minutes.
2. Show genuine interest: Focus on your partner. Ask questions. Establish eye contact.
3. Don't give unsolicited advice: When someone you care about is sad, it's natural to want to solve the issue. However, this isn't always what the other person wants. They might just want you to be a good listener or to be there for them when they need someone to cry on. Unless your partner directly asks for help, don't try to solve the issue. Your guiding principle should be "Don't do anything, just be there!"
4. Communicate your understanding: Let your partner know that you understand. Use phrases like "What a bummer, I can see why you feel that way, you're making total sense, I'm on your side" etc.
5. Take your partner's side: Show support even if you don't agree with the person's point of view. Supporting the opposition will make your spouse bitter or sad.

6. Express a "we against others" attitude: Show your partner that you are in it together if they feel alone in a difficult situation. Tell them you're both in it together.
7. Show affection
8. Validate emotions: Let your partner know that you understand how they feel. "Yeah, that is really very sad," "I can see why you'd be unhappy about that" are phrases that show you understand how they feel.

COPING WITH YOUR PARTNER'S SADNESS, FEAR AND ANGER

It is hard for some people to listen to their partner's negative emotions; this is a form of turning away. Happy couples live by the motto "The world pauses when you are in pain, and I listen." It can be hard to listen when your partner is expressing negative emotions. Most times it is because of a person's childhood. They came from homes that discouraged negativity and provided little to no consolation. Being afraid or unhappy made you a "wimp," whether you felt it or expressed it. This leads to such people learning to compartmentalize their feelings and develop into an independent problem-solver who disengage from "feelings." To have true intimacy, you need to be present for your spouse and take the time to understand how they view the world. The following advice will be helpful if you're having trouble handling your spouse's expression of emotional pain:
1. Acknowledge the difficulty: Let your partner know that dealing with and responding to unpleasant emotions is difficult for you. Your willingness to work on the problem can make a big difference in how things turn out.
2. Self-soothe: Use self-soothing techniques if your partner's emotions are too much for you to handle.
3. Remember the goal is understanding: Don't trying to solve the issue or downplay your partner's feelings. Simply pay attention to what they are saying.
4. Use exploratory statements and open-ended questions: If you want your spouse to talk, frame your answers to what they're saying as either exploratory statements or open-ended questions. These strategies show support and invite a response.

 Exploratory statements include: I want to know everything you're feeling, Nothing is more important to me right now than listening to you, We have lots of time to talk, Tell me all of your feelings and major concerns here etc.
Open-ended questions include: What are your concerns?, Can you tell me more about what you're feeling?, What do you need from me right now?, What makes this situation so difficult or stressful?, What are you most concerned about?

5. Don't ask "Why?": Avoid starting your questions with "Why?". Asking "Why?" in a conversation about how your partner is feeling comes off as criticism. A better strategy is to ask, "What makes you think that?" or "Tell me how you made that decision".

6. Bear witness: People who are depressed want to know that you care about their emotions so they won't feel alone. You can do this for your partner by bearing witness to their sorrow. This means being forward about your support for your partner, acknowledging and appreciating the experience. A great way to do this is to repeat what your spouse says in your own words.

EXTRA TIPS FOR LISTENING TO SADNESS AND CRYING

1. Ask what's missing: When someone is depressed, they believe they have lost someone or something. Sometimes what's missing will be clear but other times, it may not be so obvious. You can encourage them to talk about it by asking them about it.

2. Don't try to cheer up your partner: When someone is sad, we want to make them laugh, smile, or lift their spirits. However, unless your partner asks for it, it is more beneficial to listen to them rather than try to make them feel better.

EXTRA TIPS FOR LISTENING TO ANGER

1. Don't take it personally: Understand that your partner is not angry with you and if there were, becoming defensive wouldn't help the situation.

2. Don't ever tell your partner to calm down: It can be seen as a sign that you don't believe the anger is warranted or they shouldn't express anger. The goal is to show that you understand and accept your partner's emotions rather than to change them.

EXTRA TIP FOR LISTENING TO FEAR AND STRESS

Don't minimize it: When your partner is worried, it can be easy to minimize it when trying to reassure them. Statements like "Don't be silly" and "There's nothing to be afraid of" can look like mocking. According to Gavin de Becker in his book The Gift of Fear, the greatest way to be safe is to have an intuitive understanding of when we are dealing with a dangerous circumstance or somebody. He advises us to trust our fears rather than brush them off .

WHAT TO DO WHEN YOUR SPOUSE DOESN'T TURN TOWARD YOU

It can be very hurtful when your partner turns away from you. Couples tend to distance themselves from one another due to carelessness. They lose focus and start taking one other for granted. This is why it is important to appreciate the value of the small things and paying close attention to them. However, there can also be deeper reasons for why couples continue to miss one another. Marriage is like a dance. Sometimes you'll feel close to your partner and other times you'll want to distance yourself for some moments of independence. Some people crave independence more frequently and intensely than others but this doesn't stop their relationship from working if they can tolerate each other's differences. The best thing you can do for your marriage is to speak it out if you feel like your spouse is giving you the cold shoulder or if your spouse's idea of closeness feels like smothering to you.

THE POWER OF THE FIRST THREE PRINCIPLES
Friendship is important to a relationship's long-term viability. It is the source of PSO which is the strong energy that allows you to trust and give each other the benefit of the doubt during disagreements. A couple's friendship contributes to PSO in part by balancing the partners' levels of power so that neither feels belittled. Even if you don't agree with each other's point of view, you can typically respect and honor one another when you do so. There is usually always a lot of marital distress when there is a power imbalance.

LESSONS
1. Being supportive of one another makes your marriage stronger and passionate.
2. Couples struggle to move toward one another and build trust due to missing a bid and being distracted by technology.
3. Although you want to help your partner solve their problems, sometimes all they need is a listening ear.
4. Not bring able to listen to your partner's negative emotions is a form of turning away.
5. To have true intimacy, you need to be there for your spouse and take the time to understand how they view the world.
6. Exploratory statements and open-ended questions show support and invite a response.
7. It is important to speak up if you feel your partner is turning away from you.
8. PSO is the strong energy that allows you to trust and give each other the benefit of the doubt during disagreements.

QUESTIONS

1. How often do you have regular conversations with your spouse?

_____

_____

_____

_____

_____

_____

_____

_____

_____

_____

2. What are your views on romance?

_____

_____

_____

_____

_____

_____

_____

_____

_____

_____

_____

3. How has constant use of technology affected your relationship?

_____

_____

_____

_____

_____

_____

_____

_____

_____

_____

4. What steps have you and your partner out in place to avoid distractions from technology?

_____

_____

_____

_____

_____

_____

_____

_____

_____

_____

_____

_____

_____

5. How has your childhood experiences affected the way you deal with negative emotions?

_____

_____

_____

_____

_____

_____

_____

_____

_____

_____

_____

_____

6. What do you do when our partner expresses negative emotions?

_____

_____

7. What is your idea of closeness?

8. How have you felt belittled by your partner?

_____

_____

9. What forms of power imbalance exists in your relationship?

_____

_____

_____

_____

_____

_____

_____

_____

_____

_____

_____

_____

_____

_____

10. How can you change your reaction when your partner doesn't turn toward
    you?

_____

_____

_____

_____

_____

_____

_____

_____

_____

_____

_____

_____

_____

_____

_____

_____

CHAPTER 7: PRINCIPLE 4: LET YOUR PARTNER INFLUENCE YOU

OBJECTIVES
1. Identifying signs of resistance.
2. Understanding the importance of letting your partner influence you.
3. Being an emotionally intelligent husband.

In the Love Lab's nine-year long-term research of 130 newlywed couples, they discovered that men who allowed their spouses to influence them had better relationships and were less likely to eventually divorce than men who fought their wives' influence. A man's marriage has an 81% chance of failing if he is unable to share power with his partner. It's also important for wives to treat their husbands with respect. However, data show that most wives already do it, even in unhappy marriages. This does not mean they're never angry with their partners. It just means that they allowed their spouses to influence their choices by taking into consideration their feelings and thoughts. Most times, men don't.

"ANYTHING YOU SAY, DEAR?"
The happiest and most stable marriages are those in which the husband did not resist sharing authority and making decisions with his wife. During disagreements, these husbands actively sought a compromise as opposed to standing their ground. A man who uses one of the four horsemen to intensify a dispute is clearly fighting his wife's influence. There are some men who use the four horsemen to silence their wives rather than acknowledging her feelings. This strategy leads to an unstable marriage. Although it's important for husbands and wives to work together to prevent the four horsemen from taking control of a situation, it's important for men to understand the danger this poses to their marriage. When a wife uses the four horsemen the same way, marriages typically don't become more unstable. There is a socio-cultural explanation for this. Overly submissive wives who can't stand up to their husband's influence are prone to depression, which is terrible for both their health and their relationships. Therefore, rather than entirely giving in, it might be better for a woman to aggravate the situation. This explains why the marriage won't suffer if a wife occasionally uses one of the four horsemen to emphasize what she wants from her spouse. This show of authority evens out the power dynamics between couples. Data show that males are much more likely than their wives to escalate a marital argument by using the four horsemen. They are more likely to jeopardize their marriage when they do so.

SIGNS OF RESISTANCE

Some men are very upfront about not sharing power with their wives. There are still spouses who refuse to listen to any opinions their wives express or care about how they feel when making decisions. Some men believe they must be in charge of their marriages and, consequently, their wives. A marriage cannot succeed unless both partners respect and honor one another. Accepting influence does not mean that you should never express negative feelings toward your partner. Repressing bad feelings isn't healthy for your marriage or your blood pressure.

WHAT HUSBANDS CAN LEARN FROM WIVES

Friendship is better when couples accept each other's influence. When a guy is receptive to learning from his wife, the marriage is more enjoyable. Women can teach men a lot about friendship since they are more inclined to talk about and understand feelings. This does not mean that all women are more emotionally intelligent and have more" people skills" than all men. However, women typically possess greater emotional intelligence than their husbands for one reason: they had a head start in developing these abilities. When young boys play, the game itself is more important than their interactions or feelings. But for young girls, emotions are more important.

Girls receive a thorough education in emotions by the end of their childhood because a strong emphasis on social interactions and feelings was taught. A boy's ability to work with others and resolve conflicts amicably in games will be an asset later in the boardroom or on the construction site, but it will be a liability in marriage if it comes at the expense of understanding the emotions behind his wife's perspectives. As guys become older, they rarely play with girls, so they miss the opportunity to learn from them. Eleanor Maccoby of Stanford University discovered that while roughly 35% of best friendships in preschool are between boys and girls, by age 7, it disappears. At very young ages, boys will only allow other boys to influence them when they play, while girls allow either girls or boys to influence them. Girls get tired of this situation and quit wishing to play with boys around the age of five to seven.

EMOTIONALLY INTELLIGENT HUSBANDS

The Love Lab's research on newlywed couples shows that more husbands are transforming. The emotional intelligence of the guys they investigated is about 35%. According to research from earlier decades, the number used to be very low. An emotionally intelligent husband is willing to learn more about emotions from his wife since he respects and honors her. He might not show emotions in the same way as his wife but he will learn how to relate to her on an emotional level. The next stage in social development is the emotionally intelligent husband. An emotionally intelligent naturally incorporates the first three principles into his daily life. He shows his adoration and love for his wife and he communicates it by turning toward her in his daily acts. This is an advantage for both his marriage and his kids. According to research, a spouse who can accept advice from his wife is also likely to make a great father. He encourages his children to appreciate their own feelings and themselves since he is not afraid of emotions. This method of parenting is referred to as "emotion coaching." When parents use this parenting approach, their children benefit. This new kind of husband and father has a rich and fulfilling life. A really sad tale is the other kind of husband and father. He tends to adopt a more authoritarian stance or retreat into himself. He is searching for the respect and honor he believes is rightfully his, so he does not show others much respect or honor. He doesn't want to yield to his wife's influence because he is afraid of losing his power.

LEARNING TO YIELD

Some men struggle with the change in the husband's role. Men have always been expected to manage their families. That sense of responsibility and entitlement gets passed down from father to son in so many subtle ways. Today's couples face significant problems related to this shift in gender roles. Wives often complain that males still don't contribute fairly to household work and child care. This is a problem that affects both younger and older marriages. Men who are open to influence have successful marriages. Those who are unwilling witness the instability of their marriages. Husbands who accept influence have discovered that you have to give in or yield in order to win. If you pay attention to how you interact with your spouse, you can develop the skill of accepting influence. This means applying the first three concepts in your daily life. The key to solving issues is to be open to compromise; look through your partner's requests for something you can accept. Old habits are impossible to break overnight. But admitting that you struggle with power-sharing is a step in the right direction. The next step is to ask your partner to support you in your efforts to find a solution to this problem. Ask your partner to gently alert you to any instances where you accidentally behave in a domineering, defensive, or disrespectful manner.

LESSONS

1. Men who allow their spouses to influence them have better relationships and are less likely to divorce.
2. Accepting influence does not mean that you should never express negative feelings toward your partner.
3. An emotionally intelligent husband is willing to learn more about emotions from his wife because he respects and honors her.
4. An emotionally intelligent man is very likely to be a good father.
5. The key to solving issues is to be open to compromise.
6. Old habits are hard to break but it is important to admit that you have problem letting go of certain habits.

QUESTIONS

1. How has your spouse influenced you over time?

_____

_____

_____

_____

_____

_____

_____

_____

_____

_____

_____

2. How has your partner refused to share power with you over time?

_____

_____

_____

_____

_____

_____

_____

_____

_____

_____

_____

3. As a husband, what have you learnt from your wife?

_____

_____

_____

_____

_____

_____

_____

_____

_____

_____

4. What are the characteristics of an emotionally intelligent husband?

_____

_____

_____

_____

_____

_____

_____

_____

_____

_____

5. How did your upbringing affect your emotional intelligence?

_____

_____

_____

_____

_____

_____

_____

_____

_____

_____

6. How do you let your spouse know when they're acting negatively?

_____
_____
_____
_____
_____
_____
_____
_____
_____
_____

7. What differentiates an emotionally intelligent man from other men?

_____
_____
_____
_____
_____
_____
_____
_____
_____
_____

8. What changes did you struggle with in marriage?

_____
_____
_____
_____
_____
_____
_____
_____
_____
_____

9. What compromises have you made to make your relationship better?

_____

_____

_____

_____

_____

_____

_____

_____

_____

_____

_____

_____

10. What habits are you trying to let go of?

_____

_____

_____

_____

_____

_____

_____

_____

_____

_____

_____

_____

_____

_____

_____

_____

_____

_____

_____

CHAPTER 8: THE TWO KINDS OF MARITAL CONFLICT

OBJECTIVES
1. Signs of a gridlock.
2. Managing conflict.
3. Understanding the difference between perpetual and solvable problems.

In every relationship and marriage each person has their own beliefs and values which can cause some issues. While some confrontations are simple annoyances, others can be very complicated and dramatic. All marital conflicts fall into one of two categories: either they can be resolved, meaning they will always be a part of your lives in some way, or they are perpetual, meaning they will never go away completely.

PERPETUAL PROBLEMS
This is what happens in most marriages. The Love Lab often observed couples still fighting over the same topic at 4-year follow-ups. Here are some typical ongoing issues:
1. Donald claims he is not yet ready to have a child and is unsure if he ever will be. Meg wants to have a baby.
2. Walter wants to have sex more often than Dana.
3. Chris slacks and hardly ever contributes in house chores until Susan nags him, which enrages him.

However, despite their differences, couples can still happy in their marriages. This is because they have found a solution to their issues before they become too much to handle. Perpetual problems cause relationships to fail in unstable marriages. The couple becomes gridlocked while trying to solve their issue. When they argue, there is less humor and affection while the four horsemen are ever more present. When a couple is in a gridlock, they may try to make things better by gradually isolating the problematic area—for instance, by agreeing not to notice or bring it up. As they grow more and more entrapped in the negativity, the couple's faith in one another and the relationship gets worse. They start to think the other person is being selfish and even though they still live together, they move toward leading separate lives and will eventually feel lonely.

THE SIGNS OF GRIDLOCK
1. You feel your partner is rejecting you as a result of the conflict.
2. You keep bringing it up but don't go far.
3. You become resistant to compromise and become firmly rooted in your positions.

4. You become more irritated and hurt when you talk about the subject.
5. You don't use humor, amusement, or affection in your discussions on the issue.
6. You become even more firm in your beliefs and less inclined to compromise as a result of this vilification.
7. You eventually stop connecting emotionally with one another.

There is a way out of any kind of gridlock. All you need is drive and a willingness to look into the problems fueling the gridlock. You can do this by identifying your most important personal dreams for your life and talk about them with your partner. Unfulfilled dreams are the root of every gridlocked disagreement. The never-ending issue is a sign of a huge difference between the two of you that must be resolved before the issue can be resolved.

SOLVABLE PROBLEMS

They are less complicated than perpetual problems but they can be painful. Even when a problem is solvable, it may not always be solved. The fifth rule of marriage success addresses solvable issues head-on.

TELLING THE DIFFERENCE

It can be hard to know if the problem you have with your partner is solvable or gridlocked. Solvable problems issues are less dramatic than perpetual ones. With solvable issues, you only have one issue in mind. There isn't a deeper issue driving your conflict. For Rachel and Jason, arguing over speeding is a solvable issue. They travel to and fro together each morning from their suburban home to Pittsburgh's downtown. She believes he speeds. But for him, he must drive quickly because it takes her so long to get dressed and he doesn't want to be at work late. According to Rachel, he takes a long time to shower first which is why it takes her so long in the morning. This couple's trouble with speeding is a solvable issue. It is situational; it only happens as they are leaving for work, and it has no impact on other aspects of their lives. Their disagreements are just about speeding and their morning routine. They could easily reach a compromise if they learned how to communicate with one another more effectively. However, they will become more resentful and firm in their positions if they can't come to an agreement on the matter. It can develop into a persistent, gridlocked issue.

THE KEYS TO MANAGING CONFLICT

1. Negative emotions are important: It can be difficult to hear your partner's negative emotions but it is important to know about them. Negative feelings can teach us valuable lessons about how to love one another more. These

conversations can be hard for both sides. Recognizing this and remembering to be kind to one another will help.

2. No one is right: In marital disagreement; there is no absolute reality. According to Dan Siegel, there is no perfect perception. If you keep this fundamental truth in mind, it will help you in settling your disagreements.

3. Acceptance is crucial: it is hard for people to take advice unless they feel appreciated, accepted, and understood for who they are. People can't change when they feel disapproved of, or unappreciated. Make sure your partner feels valued before you urge them to change. You need to show your spouse that you accept them if you want to develop your connection.

4. Focus on fondness and admiration: Focus more on the activities that build fondness and admiration if you or your partner finds it hard to understand each other's point of view. Maintaining a happy marriage depends on a strong system of fondness and appreciation.

Some couples have the ability to understand their partner's flaws. So, although they express to one another every feeling on the emotional spectrum, they also express their basic affection and respect for one another. They communicate to one another that they are liked and accepted. When couples can't accomplish this, it's easy to hold grudges. You must forgive one another and put aside your grudges from the past if you want your marriage to continue happily. It can be challenging, but it is definitely worth it.

LESSONS
1. Conflicts and issues happen in marriages even happy ones; it's normal.
2. Marital conflicts are either solvable or perpetual.
3. It is important to address solvable issues head-on.
4. Negative feelings teach us valuable lessons about how to love one another more.
5. To build a connection with your partner you need to show them you accept them.
6. Build fondness and admiration with your partner, it helps you understand each other.
7. Although gridlocks are very hard, they can be gotten out of with determination and willingness.

QUESTIONS
1. What flaws does your partner have?

_____

_____

_____

_____

_____

_____

_____

_____

_____

_____

_____

_____

2. What are the categories of marital conflicts?

_____

_____

_____

_____

_____

_____

_____

_____

_____

_____

3. What's the difference between solvable and perpetual problems?

_____

_____

_____

_____

_____

_____

_____

_____

_____

_____

_____

4. What solvable problem do you currently have in your marriage?

_____

_____

_____

_____

_____

_____

_____

_____

_____

_____

_____

5. What are your most important personal dreams?

_____

_____

_____

_____

_____

_____

_____

_____

_____

_____

_____

_____

_____

6. How do you feel when your partner discusses their negative emotions with you?

_____
_____
_____
_____
_____
_____
_____
_____
_____
_____
_____
_____

7. What unfulfilled dreams do you have?

_____
_____
_____
_____
_____
_____
_____
_____
_____
_____
_____

8. What solvable issues have become gridlocked in your marriage?

_____
_____
_____
_____
_____
_____
_____
_____

9. What grudges do you hold against your partner?

10. What are the signs of a gridlock?

CHAPTER 9: PRINCIPLE 5: SOLVE YOUR SOLVABLE PROBLEMS

OBJECTIVES
1. Softening your start-up.
2. Knowing when to stop.
3. Making your repair attempts visible.

The fifth principle and model for resolving conflict in a happy relationship has the following steps:
1. Soften your start-up.
2. Learn to make and receive repair attempts.
3. Soothe yourself and each other.
4. Compromise.
5. Process any grievances so that they don't linger.

This principle is basically about having good manners. It is about treating your partner with the same respect you show others.

STEP 1: SOFTEN YOUR START-UP
Wives are more likely to bring up a sensitive subject and push for a solution and this isn't good. Husbands usually want to avoid confronting difficult issues. This is due to physiological factors. Men experience floods far more frequently so they are more likely to avoid conflict. However, there is a difference in how a wife starts difficult conversations with her husband. Only 40% of marriages end in divorce because of frequent arguments. Most times, marriages fail because the husband and wife distance themselves from one another so much that their friendship and sense of connection are lost. Research on repair by Jani Driver and Amber Tabares discovered that accepting some responsibility for the issue is an important component of soft start-up. The best soft start-up has four parts:
1. I share some responsibility for this …
2. Here's how I feel …
3. about a specific situation and …
4. here's what I need

A soft start-up doesn't need to be overly diplomatic in order to be successful but it must be free of criticism and disdain. The key to preventing a harsh start-up is for both partners to collaborate on the first four principles. If you do this, the wife's start-up will naturally soften. Make sure your partner feels known, respected, and loved by you and that you are willing to accept their influence if they have a tendency to bring up topics angrily. If you are the one who initiates more harsh start-ups in your relationship, you must soften up if you want your marriage to succeed. If you're upset with your spouse, take a deep breath and think about the best way to bring up the issue. Avoid talking about the subject altogether until you have calmed down if you are too upset. Here are some steps you can take to calm down:

1. Make statements that start with "I" instead of "You.": Instead of saying "I'd like for you to listen to me," say "You are not listening to me." "I want us to save more" instead of "You are irresponsible with money." Your conversation will more successful if they focus on how you feel rather than on accusing your partner.
2. Describe what is happening. Don't evaluate or judge: Just tell your partner what you observe so they won't feel attacked.
3. Be clear about your positive needs: Your partner can't read your mind to know what you need; you have to let them know.
4. Be polite: Use expressions like 'please' and 'I'd like it if'.
5. Be appreciative.
6. Don't store things up: Don't wait too long to bring up a problem, it will only get worse in your mind.

Once you start to soften your start-ups, don't expect your partner to immediately respond with great sweetness and cooperation. They might still be expecting criticism. Don't escalate the conflict by giving up.

STEP 2: LEARN TO MAKE AND RECEIVE REPAIR ATTEMPTS

It is important knowing when to stop; end conversations that start off poorly, it saves you from a lot of disasters. This can be done by using repair attempts. Stable, emotionally intelligent marriages are different from others because repair attempts reach the other person. This is because there is no negativity between them.

GETTING THE MESSAGE THROUGH

A relationship's status determines if a repair attempt is successful. Couples send and receive repair attempts easily in happy marriages. You don't have to wait for things to become better in your marriage before you start listening to each other's repair attempts. Start today by paying close attention and teach each other to recognize them when they are directed in your direction. The best approach is to make your repair attempt very visible especially if your relationship is in negativity. You can formalize repair attempts by using these pre-written sentences. Some examples are;

I FEEL

1. I'm getting scared.

2. Please say that more gently.
3. Did I do something wrong?
4. That hurt my feelings.
5. I'm feeling sad.

I NEED TO CALM DOWN

1. I need things to be calmer right now.
2. I need your support right now.
3. Just listen to me right now and try to understand.
4. Tell me you love me.
5. Can I have a kiss?
6. Can I take that back?
7. This is important to me. Please listen.

SORRY

1. Let me try again.
2. I want to be gentler toward you right now, and I don't know how.
3. Tell me what you hear me saying.
4. How can I make things better?
5. Let's try that over again.

GET TO YES

1. You're starting to convince me.
2. I agree with part of what you're saying.
3. Let's compromise here.
4. Let's find our common ground.
5. I never thought of things that way.

STOP ACTION!

1. I might be wrong here.
2. Please, let's stop for a while.
3. Let's take a break.
4. I'm feeling flooded.
5. Please stop.

I APPRECIATE

1. I know this isn't your fault.
2. My part of this problem is …
3. I see your point.
4. Thank you for …
5. That's a good point.

Pick a low-intensity disagreement to talk about. Each person gets 15 minutes to speak. Make sure you use a term from the list at least once during the conversation. Let your spouse know in advance if you're going to try a repair. You should also accept it when your partner announces a repair attempt. See it as an effort to improve the situation.

STEP 3: SOOTHE YOURSELF AND EACH OTHER
Conflict discussions, however, might cause floods in unstable relationships. You feel overburdened both physically and emotionally when this happens. Your body is in distress in the meantime. Usually, you're sweating, your heart is racing, and you're holding your breath. In most instances, when one spouse doesn't understand the other's repair attempt, it's because the listener is drowning out the other spouse's words and can't actually hear them.

STEP 4: COMPROMISE
The only way to fix marital issues is through compromise. When couples can't reach a compromise, it's because they approached it wrongly. Negotiation is only possible after softening the start-up, repairing your discussion, and remaining composed. Compromise is more than just one individual changing. Negotiating and working out mutually beneficial compromises are important. If you don't accept your partner's shortcomings, you won't be able to compromise. Instead, you'll be wishing for things and wishing "if only". "If only" makes you angry about what you don't have while cherishing builds gratitude for what you have. Conflicts will be very hard to resolve if you have the "if only" mindset. Remember, accepting influence is the cornerstone of any compromise. In order for a compromise to be successful, you cannot be indifferent to your spouse's ideas and preferences. You don't have to agree on everything but you do need to be willing to give your partner's views some thought. This is really what embracing influence is all about. Men typically find it more difficult to accept influence from their wives but regardless of your gender, a lack of open-mindedness is a serious disadvantage when it comes to resolving disputes. Let your partner know if you don't see things from their point of view. Ask questions to help you understand better.

STEP 5: DEALING WITH EMOTIONAL INJURIES
You avoid a destructive conflict when you can reach a compromise on a solvable issue in a way that makes you both happy. Even if you are able to get past the reasons that led to these disputes, they can still be painful to overcome. This harm is called an "emotional injury. If emotional wounds aren't healed, they can become annoyances. We all need to "process" or talk about old emotional wounds. Repressing it will just make things worse.

LESSONS

1. Marriages fail because the husband and wife distance themselves from one another and sense of connection is lost.
2. A relationship's status determines if a repair attempt is successful or not.
3. Issues will not be fixed if everyone stands their ground; it is important to compromise.
4. You have to accept your partner's shortcomings to be able to compromise.
5. It is important to let your partner know if you don't understand their point of view.
6. You should talk about your emotional wounds with your partner; it will help them understand you better and resolve issues.

QUESTIONS

1. What are the characteristics of a soft start-up?

2. Who has more harsh start-ups between you and your partner and why?

3. How do you calm down when you're angry?

_____
_____
_____
_____
_____
_____
_____
_____
_____
_____
_____

4. What makes a compromise work?

_____
_____
_____
_____
_____
_____
_____
_____
_____
_____

5. How has making compromises in the past helped your relationship?

_____
_____
_____
_____
_____
_____
_____

_____
_____
_____
_____
_____

6. What emotional wounds do you have currently?

_____
_____
_____
_____
_____
_____
_____
_____
_____
_____

7. How do you resolve conflicts with your spouse?

_____
_____
_____
_____
_____
_____
_____
_____
_____
_____
_____
_____

8. How have your emotional wounds affected your relationship?

_____
_____
_____
_____
_____
_____
_____
_____
_____
_____
_____
_____
_____
_____
_____
_____
_____
_____
_____
_____
_____
_____
_____
_____
_____
_____

CHAPTER 10: COPING WITH TYPICAL SOLVABLE PROBLEMS

OBJECTIVES
1. Dealing with money problems.
2. Changing your marriage in the right direction after childbirth.
3. Overcoming sexual issues.

Work stress, in-laws, money, sex, housework, a new baby: these are the most typical sources of marital conflict. These problems also happen in happy relationships. For a marriage to develop and deepen, spouses must work together to complete a number of emotional duties. Couples need to develop a deep understanding of one another so that they can both feel comfortable and secure in their relationship. No problem-solving expertise can resolve a perpetual conflict. Only when you both feel at ease with your differences will the tension start to reduce. But when a problem is solvable, the best approach is to find a solution. Here are seven potential issues with the task each one represents for a marriage and specific suggestions for resolving the arguments they frequently lead to.

UNPLUGGING FROM DISTRACTIONS
THE TASK: Maintaining intimacy and connection in the face of the internet age. According to a research in Los Angeles, young working couples spend an average of 35 minutes talking to each other in a week and their conversations revolve around running errands. There are different reasons for the lack of communication but constant interruptions by technology and the Internet plays a huge role.

THE SOLUTION

Even if you disagree, take your partner's complain about your technological use seriously. Every couple should create etiquette guidelines that work for them. Such guidelines should at the very least prohibit texting or checking email while eating, on a date, or when you both need to talk. You may also want to establish strict privacy guidelines. It's important to create rules that feel fair to you both and then to uphold them.

THE PROBLEM WITH PORN
Research shows constant porn use harms the nature and quality of sex in relationships—especially when a partner is watching porn alone. The effects of constantly masturbating to porn include: Less frequent sex, less sexual communication and increased risk of betrayal. Porn will always be popular and inviting, so couples should discuss their opinions and issues with it to prevent any form of betrayal.

STRESS AND MORE STRESS

THE TASK: Making your marriage a place of peace

Work stress has become a bigger contributor to marital dissatisfaction. Couples today work more than they did 30 years ago. There is no time available for socializing, unwinding, eating, and even sleeping.

THE SOLUTION

Realize that you might need some alone time to unwind after a stressful day before engaging with one another. Try not to take it personally if your spouse answers your question "What's wrong?" in a bad way or if they don't want to talk. They probably just had a bad day. Letting it go will also stop you from making the problem worse. Put some relaxation time in your schedule. Make it a tradition.

RELATIONS WITH IN-LAWS

THE TASK: Creating a sense of solidarity or "we-ness"

This typically happens between the wife and mother-in-law especially when they have very different views, thoughts and hobbies. Going out to dinner can lead to arguments. Then, there are the more important questions of values, lifestyle etc. The root of the conflict is a turf war for the husband's love. Meanwhile, the man only wishes that the two women would get along better. He does not want to have to pick between them because he loves them both.

THE SOLUTION

The husband must support his wife against his mother in order to resolve this gridlock. It is important that he creates a sense of "we-ness". The husband must let his mother know that his wife comes first. He is first a husband, then a son. His mother will be hurt but he must be firm and she will eventually come to terms with it. If she doesn't, he must remain firm for his marriage to succeed. This doesn't mean that a man should dishonor his parents or violates his core moral principles. He must, however, stand next to his wife. Not tolerating any disrespect toward your spouse from your parents is an important part of putting your spouse first and creating this sense of solidarity.

MONEY, MONEY, MONEY

THE TASK: Balancing the security and trust that money represents

Many couples have conflict over money no matter their financial status. Money represents different emotional demands like safety and power, and it is important to each person's personal value system. The secret to solving this issue is to first understand the role of a marriage in this area. Money can buy security and pleasure. We have different views about money and value, balancing these two economic realities can be hard. As a marriage progresses, this problem either gets better or worse.

THE SOLUTION

Budgeting is important. There are some easy steps you can take to figure out how much money you want to spend and on what. The most important thing for your marriage in terms of money matters is that you communicate your needs, wants, and dreams to one another before coming up with a strategy. Make sure your budget doesn't mean any of you suffers. You'll each need to be tough about topics that you consider non-negotiable.

STEP 1: ITEMIZE YOUR CURRENT EXPENDITURE

Use a form to document your financial activities throughout the past month; six months, or year, depending on what period best suits your needs. You can do this by looking at your financial accounts.

STEP 2: MANAGE EVERYDAY FINANCES

1. List every expenditure that you believe is necessary for your pleasure and wellbeing.
2. Take a close look at your assets and income. Work on developing a budget that will allow you to manage your regular spending and live within your means.
3. Create a strategy for regularly paying your bills. Decide who is in charge of doing that.
4. Talk about your individual to-do lists and plans with one another. Find areas where your two methods can coexist. Choose a practical plan that enables both of you to meet your basic demands. Review it every few months.

STEP 3: PLAN YOUR FINANCIAL FUTURE

1. Think about how your life will be in 5, 10, 20, or 30 years. Consider your ideal lifestyle, the things you want and the financial disasters you would most like to avoid.
2. Make a list of your long-term financial goals.
3. Exchange lists. Look for similarities in your long-term goals. Talk about your views.
4. Develop a long-term financial strategy that will allow you both to achieve your goals. Make sure you review this strategy periodically.

HOUSEWORK

THE TASK: Building a spirit of fairness and cooperation.

Men underestimate how much women care about maintaining order in their homes. A wife feels insulted and abandoned when her husband doesn't do his share of the housework. This causes bitterness and an unhappy marriage. However, the men don't do it intentionally; they just don't understand why housework is so important to their wives. Another thing that contributes to this is how they were brought up. Many people were raised in families where their father didn't help with the chores, even if their mother worked. So, on some level many men see housework as a woman's responsibility.

THE SOLUTION

Men have to do more housework. Women find it romantic. However, men slack due to lack of motivation. In relationships where the wife feels her husband is doing his share, both the husband and wife report having more fulfilling sex lives. The women in these relationships also have lower heart rates during marital disputes, which make them less likely to open a conversation rudely. Couples should discuss how much housework each person should do. Make a list to show one another your view of how things are being handled at the moment and then how you would like them to be.

BECOMING PARENTS

THE TASK: Including your children in your sense of "we-ness"

Having a child will definitely make your marriage different. According to Nora Ephron in Heartburn, it's not necessarily better or worse, it's just different. A baby causes a marriage to undergo fundamental changes. Unfortunately, those adjustments are typically for the worse.

It is entirely dependent on whether the husband transitions into motherhood alongside his wife or is left behind. Having a baby triggers a change in the new mother. A new mother almost always goes through a complete reorientation of her life's significance. She learns she is prepared to make significant sacrifices for her child. She is in awe and wonder at how strongly she feels about her baby. If the husband doesn't undergo the same life-changing experience with her, space would grow between them. The husband might still want a "just the two of us" feeling while the wife is embracing a new feeling of "we-ness" that includes their child. Following her into her new universe is the solution to his problem. This prevents him from harboring resentment toward his child. He now also feels like a parent, not just a husband. When it comes to his children, he feels protective, compassionate, and proud. How can a married couple make sure that the husband changes with his wife? The couple should spend time without the baby to concentrate on their marriage and other interests. The couple should occasionally take a break from the child. Here are some suggestions to keep couples connected once they become parents:

1. Focus on your marital friendship: Make sure you truly understand one another and your different worlds before the baby arrives. The change will be simpler the more you're a team.

2. Don't exclude Dad from baby care: Mothers tend to take over when they give birth. Some men are okay with standing aside and letting this happen. However, this makes them do less and less, reducing their accomplishments and confidence in raising their own child. Eventually, they start to feel excluded. The solution is easy; the mother needs to back off. If she disagrees with her husband's methods, she should keep in mind that the infant is also his child and will gain from exposure to other parenting philosophies.

3. Carve out time for the two of you: Making marriage a priority is a necessary part of the transition to motherhood. Spend some quality time alone with each other; hire a babysitter, a family member, or a friend. You have succeeded if you end up talking about the baby a lot on your dates. Your talks when you're alone together won't always focus on your child as the baby grows.

4. Be sensitive to Dad's needs: The man is still going to feel somewhat deprived by the baby's constant need for his wife, even if he is a good team player. Even though he knows that the baby's needs come before his own, he will miss his wife. He will be more understanding and encouraging if his wife expresses to him how much she still values what he has sacrificed and how important he still is in her life.

5. Give Mom a break: Whether a woman is working or the baby is her full-time job, she is likely to be tired even though she's happy about her new motherhood experiences. Try to create breaks for her to do other things and focus on her.

SEX

THE TASK: Basic respect and acceptance of one another

So many couples complain about the lack of romance. In most cases, the husband has more sex cravings than the wife. Even among happy couples, the husbands seek more sexual intercourse. What makes a long-term relationship sexually satisfying? In a study of couples with young children, it was discovered that those who had good to great sex lives prioritized sex instead of seeing it as the last task on a long list of duties. They also made sure to spend alone time together. They were attentive to each other both inside and outside of the bedroom and had a great level of trust for one another. The secret to long-term fulfillment, both sexually and otherwise, is to value and encourage the friendship between couples. When you apply the lessons of the Seven Principles to your daily lives, your sex life is likely to get better. The conversation between a husband and wife regarding their sexual desires tend to be indirect, vague, and unsatisfying because they find it uncomfortable to talk about. One of the most enjoyable ways to communicate with one another and increase intimacy is through sex. Tension-filled conversations can lead to irritation and hurt feelings.

THE SOLUTION

Learn how to discuss sex with each other in a way that makes each partner feel secure. The two of you will have a better time if you do this. Research shows that when partners feel comfortable discussing this subject, women experience more orgasms.

FIVE WAYS TO MAKE SEX MORE PERSONAL AND ROMANTIC

1. Redefine what you mean by sex: Relationship counseling books are usually put in a different section from books about sex. The latter are called "sex manuals," and they can discuss anatomy and physiology in great detail but they never discuss sex in terms of relationships. Relationship books also don't address sex directly. Sexual anxiety happens when sex becomes more about technique than passion and communication. Men are concerned with their erections. Women stress over experiencing orgasm. It is awkward to discuss sex when both parties feel self-conscious. Separate sex from the rest of your relationship. Stop thinking that sex is all about orgasm and start seeing all your positive interactions as sex. Every time you turn toward each other in any way throughout the day, you are engaging in foreplay. Couples can see that sex is all about connection when they don't make orgasm the goal.

2. Learn how to talk about it: Couples want to talk about their sex life but they struggle to do so without coming off as judgmental or self-conscious. So, the following are some guidelines:

● Be gentle and positive: Don't criticize your partner because most people feel so vulnerable about whether they are attractive to their spouse and being a good lover. Discuss potential improvements while coming up with new ideas.

● Compromise: You and your partner should decide what feels secure and safe. Sexuality is flexible; accommodate each other's preferences in ways that are enjoyable for both of you.

3. Chart your sexual love maps: What felt good the last time? What do you need to make sex better?
4. Learn how to initiate sex and to refuse it gently: Many couples find it awkward to talk about how to initiate sex and struggle with letting their partner know they're not in the mood. Being rejected is difficult to handle. Have a ritual for managing sex in your relationship that makes "yes" and "no" feel less loaded. A ritual is an approach that you both anticipate, know you can rely on, and relish. It makes asking for sex obvious.

Here are some rituals practiced by couples:
- Out rightly saying, "I want to make love."
- Asking your spouse if they want to make love while putting your arms around them.
- Sending a daytime erotic text or email to the partner.
- Suggesting a bath together.

REFUSING SEX GENTLY

If you're not feeling it, gently break the news to your partner. Say to them in your own words;
- "I'm not in the mood at all right now. You are still incredibly beautiful to me, though."
- "I'm sorry, honey, but this is not the moment for me to make love to you. However, I still love you deeply and think you are gorgeous."

COPING WITH "NO"

It is important that you don't punish your partner for saying no to sex. However, it is easier said than done. When the wife does it, the husband tends to react in a hurt, frustrated, or even angry manner. The more you can hear, understand, and appreciate your partner's "no" regarding any marital issue, the more "yes" there will be in your relationship.

LESSONS
1. Not tolerating any disrespect toward your spouse from your parents is a way of putting your spouse first and creating a sense of solidarity.
2. Money represents different emotional demands.
3. Having a child always changes a marriage but it is important that you work with your partner so it changes for the better instead of worse.
4. The secret to long-term fulfillment, sexually and otherwise, is to value and encourage the friendship between couples.

5. Sexual anxiety happens when sex becomes more about technique than passion and communication.
6. A ritual is an approach that you anticipate, know you can rely on, and relish.

QUESTIONS
1. What causes most of your marital conflict?

_____
_____
_____
_____
_____
_____
_____
_____
_____
_____
_____
_____
_____
_____

2. How do you unwind after a long day?

_____
_____
_____
_____
_____
_____
_____
_____
_____
_____
_____
_____
_____
_____

3. What do you do with your spouse during your free time?

_____
_____
_____

_____
_____
_____
_____
_____
_____
_____
_____
_____
_____

4. What kind of relationship do you have with your in-laws?

_____
_____
_____
_____
_____
_____
_____
_____
_____
_____
_____

5. What are your long term financial goals?

_____
_____
_____
_____
_____
_____
_____
_____
_____
_____
_____

6. How did giving birth affect you and your marriage?

_____

_____

_____

_____

_____

_____

_____

_____

_____

_____

_____

7. What is your current sex life like?

_____

_____

_____

_____

_____

_____

_____

_____

_____

_____

_____

8. How did you change after you had a child?

_____

_____

_____

_____

_____

_____

_____

_____

_____

_____

_____

_____

_____

9. How do you refuse sex with your partner?

_____

_____

_____

_____

_____

_____

_____

_____

_____

_____

_____

_____

10. In what ways have you felt punished for saying no to sex?

_____

_____

_____

_____

_____

_____

_____

_____

_____

_____

_____

_____

_____

_____

CHAPTER 11: PRINCIPLE 6: OVERCOME GRIDLOCK

OBJECTIVES
1. Respecting your partner's dreams.
2. Knowing when you've reached a gridlock.

Some irreconcilable differences exist in every relationship but gridlock only happens when partners can't find a solution to these perpetual differences. They see the other person as self-centered and this makes compromise impossible. Arguments can be about very important or minor things. You've reached gridlock if:
1. You've had the same argument multiple times without coming to a conclusion.
2. None of you respond to the situation with humor, empathy, or love.
3. The topic is becoming more divisive over time.
4. Making a compromise seems impossible.

Avoiding gridlock is the best way to deal with it. Conflicts that would have overwhelmed you in the past become easier to address as you get to know and trust each other. When couples are able to avoid conflict, they start to treat their perpetual issues as a bothersome backache. They know the challenge will never go away, but they prevent it from dominating their lives. You don't have to find a solution to the issue to get past gridlock. The goal is to be able to recognize and discuss the problem without hurting one another.

WHAT DREAMS ARE MADE OF
A gridlock is a sign that each of you has goals for your life that the other doesn't know about, acknowledge or respect. Dreams are the aspirations and desires that make up your identity and give your life direction and meaning. Dreams can function on a variety of levels. They can be insightful, while others are really useful. A dream can be problematic if you hide it from your partner or they don't respect it. In some situations, the conflict may be openly fought over, or it may be hidden and only conveyed symbolically.

WHEN DREAMS ARE RESPECTED
Why do some couples handle these kinds of problems so effortlessly while others struggle? Happy couples know about each other's goals and see supporting one another as one of the goals of marriage. Partners in fulfilling relationships take into account each other's aspirations while defining what their marriage is all about. These goals may be as specific or intangible.

BECOME A DREAM DETECTIVE

You need to determine which dream or dreams are causing disputes in your marriage if you've reached a deadlock on any matter, no matter how big or minor. It is obvious you're struggling with a secret dream if you blame your partner for the problems in your marriage. It could mean that because it is hidden, you are unaware of your role in starting the conflict. Finding a secret dream is difficult but the dream won't appear until you feel comfortable discussing it in your marriage. Start by focusing on the first three principles in order to develop a closer bond with your partner. Deeply personal dreams don't have to be private or hidden in order for your relationship to work. Some partners don't feel that they have a right to pursue their goals. They sometimes see their own desires as childish or impractical but this doesn't stop to the need. Basically, when you bury a dream, it reappears in a hidden manner as a standoff.

WORKING ON A GRIDLOCKED MARITAL ISSUE

Solving these problems will take time. The issues might get worse rather than better when you first start to identify and recognize your dreams. Be tolerant. It takes courage to acknowledge your dreams and fight for them.

STEP 1: EXPLORE THE DREAMS

To get started, identify a particular gridlocked conflict to work on and write down an explanation for your position. Never criticize your spouse. Pay attention to what each partner wants, needs, and feels about the circumstance. Describe the origin of these dreams and why they have such significance for you. Once you both realize whose dreams are causing the gridlock, it's time to talk about them. Each member has 15-minutes to speak and listen. Don't try to solve the issue. Your goal is to understand why you each have such strong opinions on this matter.

- Speaker's job: Honestly discuss your views and what it means to you. Describe the origin of the dream and what it means. Be honest and upfront about what you want and why it matters so much. Don't try to downplay your feelings regarding your dream.
- Listener's job: Don't judge. Although your dream conflicts with your spouse's, don't take it personally. Don't waste time coming up with counter arguments or solutions. All you need to do is listen to your spouse's dream and encourage them.

STEP 2: SOOTHE

Keep an eye on how each of you responds to the conversation. In case you start to feel stressed, let your partner know. If flooding occurs, the conversation won't progress. If any of you get angry, make sure to use repair attempts. If flooding happens, take a break for at least 20 minutes, and do something calming during that time.

STEP 3: REACH A TEMPORARY COMPROMISE

Realize that the goal is not to end the issue; it probably won't ever be fully resolved. Instead, the goal is to make the problem harmless, to try to remove the hurt so that the issue stops being a significant source of grief. You should start this approach by looking for common ground. Find the absolute minimums you will not budge on. To do this, you need to dig deep into your heart and try to split the issue into two categories:

- Non-negotiable areas: These are the conflict-related issues that you just cannot compromise on without compromising your fundamental requirements or core principles.
- Areas of flexibility: These are all aspects of the problem that you can be flexible with. Make this category as big as you can.

Your spouse should see both of your lists. Come up with a temporary compromise by working together. Try it out for about two months, and then assess your progress. This makes life a little bit easier for you both not solve the issue.

STEP 4: SAY "THANK YOU"

It can take more than one session to break the gridlock on problems that have caused your marriage great distress. No matter how much you work to accept one other's points of view without passing judgment, these sessions can still be unpleasant. Recapturing the spirit of thankfulness is the goal but it can be tough to accomplish after talking about gridlocked marital issues. Offer your companion three specific thanks so you can go out on a high note. You'll know you're making progress when the issue in question feels less heavy, when you can talk about it while maintaining your sense of humor, and when it no longer crowds out the love and joy in your relationship.

LESSONS

1. Irreconcilable differences exist in every relationship.
2. Dreams are the aspirations and desires that make up your identity and give your life direction and meaning.
3. Deeply personal dreams don't have to be private or hidden for the relationship to work.
4. Always be open about how you feel when having conversations about each other's dreams.
5. Solving gridlocked issues take time; be patient.

QUESTIONS

1. What irreconcilable differences currently exist in your marriage?

_____
_____
_____
_____
_____
_____
_____
_____
_____
_____
_____
_____
_____

2. How do you know when you've reached a gridlock?

_____
_____
_____
_____
_____
_____
_____
_____
_____
_____
_____
_____
_____

3. What are your current dreams?

_____
_____
_____
_____
_____
_____
_____

_____
_____
_____
_____
_____
_____

4. What do you know about your partner's goals and aspirations?

_____
_____
_____
_____
_____
_____
_____
_____
_____
_____
_____
_____

5. How are your dreams different from your partner's dream?

_____
_____
_____
_____
_____
_____
_____
_____
_____
_____
_____

6. What hidden dreams do you have?

_____
_____
_____
_____
_____
_____
_____
_____
_____
_____
_____
_____

7. What are your non-negotiable areas?

_____
_____
_____
_____
_____
_____
_____
_____
_____
_____
_____
_____
_____
_____
_____

8. How do you overcome gridlocked issues?

_____
_____
_____

_____
_____
_____
_____
_____
_____
_____
_____
_____
_____
_____

9. Which dreams have you had to let go of in the past due to relationships?

_____
_____
_____
_____
_____
_____
_____
_____
_____
_____
_____
_____
_____
_____
_____
_____
_____
_____
_____
_____
_____
_____
_____
_____

CHAPTER 12: PRINCIPLE 7: CREATE SHARED MEANING

OBJECTIVES
1. Creating shared meaning.
2. The pillars of shared meaning.

Your marriage is probably stable and happy if you follow the first six guidelines. But a stronger sense of shared meaning is the final step. Making love and sharing duties aren't the only aspects of marriage. It can also include a spiritual component which includes developing a shared inner life, a culture full of symbols and rituals, and an appreciation for the roles and goals that unite you and help you come to terms with who you are as a family. When we think of culture, we think of large ethnic groups or even nations where certain traditions and foods are prevalent. However, two people who have decided to live together can develop a culture. Each marriage and family develops its own micro-culture. Just like other cultures, these small groups have their own myths—the stories the couple tells themselves whether true or false that explain their sense of what their marriage is like and what it means to be a part of their group as well as customs. Creating a culture doesn't mean that a couple completely agrees on all of their life principles. In its place, there is connection. They find a way to recognize each other's dreams even though they don't always share them. Each person's dream is included into the society that they create together. It can also change as a husband and wife mature. Conflict reduces and perpetual problems are less likely to result in deadlock when a couple has this shared sense of purpose. It is possible to have a healthy marriage without having a strong sense of what is truly meaningful about your life together. Even if your dreams don't line up, your marriage can still work. It is important to accept that you each have certain dreams that the other person doesn't share but can respect. Maintaining peace in a marriage is not the only important factor; your marriage will be richer, deeper, and easier the more you can agree on the essentials of life. Your connection will be deeper, richer, and more fulfilling the more shared meaning you can find. You'll also be improving the friendship in your marriage. This makes resolving any issues simpler.

THE FOUR PILLARS OF SHARED MEANING
PILLAR 1: RITUALS OF CONNECTION
Most families rarely eat dinner. This prevents good conversations during dinner and a solution is creating rituals in your family with your spouse and children. A ritual is an organized activity or habit that you all look forward to and depend on

which reflects and strengthens your sense of community. Most of us have rituals from our childhood such as attending Midnight Mass on Christmas Eve, sharing pumpkin pie with Grandma on Thanksgiving but people tend to keep the meanings behind these rituals to themselves. The rituals you individually bring to your relationship and the new ones you build together have lasting worth and significance, which strengthens your sense of family. Rituals don't always have to come from your own upbringings and family histories. You can make your own. Rituals of connection are characterized by their orderliness. They are structured, scripted traditions that you can depend on. It allows you and your partner to pay close attention to one another and establish a genuine connection. Sexual intercourse can also be a ritual if planned well.

PILLAR 2: SUPPORT FOR EACH OTHER'S ROLES
Our perception of our place in the world depends on the many roles we play. When it comes to marriage, how we see both our own and our partner's roles can either strengthen the sense of purpose and harmony between us or lead to conflict. If you and your spouse have similar expectations of one another in terms of their role in your family, your marriage will feel more complete. A marriage has more meaning when both partners share the same parenting philosophies. Your marriage will be strengthened based on how similarly you both feel the same way about certain topics. This does not mean that you have to agree on all intellectual or spiritual matters.

PILLAR 3: SHARED GOALS
The goals we work to achieve are a big part of what gives life purpose. We all have deeper, more spiritual goals in addition to some practical goals. We tend to avoid talking about our deepest aspirations. Sometimes, we haven't even asked ourselves these questions. However, once we get going, it gives us the chance to look into something that could have a significant impact on both our marriage and ourselves. By expressing your greatest goals with your spouse, you make your relationship more intimate and help to deepen your relationship.

PILLAR 4: SHARED VALUES AND SYMBOLS
The third pillar of a marriage's shared meaning is its values and beliefs. These are the philosophical principles that should direct how you spend your lives. Some people's moral principles are firmly founded in their religious beliefs. Non-religious couples also have a set of beliefs that shape their outlook on life and guide their decision-making.

Symbols, which could be material things or intangible ideas, are used to show a couple's shared morals and worldviews. A couple can openly exhibit religious symbols of religion in their house, like a crucifix. If their meaning is discussed, specific, and agreed upon, they represent values. However, there are also more customized symbols. Abstract symbols also play an important role in a marriage. Even the physical home itself might have deep symbolic significance for a marriage. A couple might see it as more than just a place to sleep and eat. Family stories also tend to be symbolic and represent deeply rooted values.

LESSONS

1. Marriage is more than making love and sharing duties; it has a spiritual component.
2. Creating a culture doesn't mean you'll agree on every life principle.
3. The rituals you individually bring to your relationship strengthen your sense of family.
4. Expressing your greatest goals with your spouse makes your relationship more intimate.

QUESTIONS

1. What are the pillars of shared meaning?

_____

_____

_____

_____

_____

_____

_____

_____

_____

_____

_____

_____

2. What micro-culture was developed in your marriage?

_____

_____

_____

_____
_____
_____
_____
_____
_____
_____
_____
_____

3. What are your deepest goals?

_____
_____
_____
_____
_____
_____
_____
_____
_____
_____
_____
_____
_____

4. What abstract symbols are important in your marriage?

_____
_____
_____
_____
_____
_____
_____
_____
_____
_____
_____
_____
_____

5. What dreams do you have that is different from that of your spouse?

_____
_____
_____
_____
_____
_____
_____
_____
_____
_____
_____

6. What rituals did your family practice during your childhood?

_____
_____
_____
_____
_____
_____
_____
_____
_____
_____
_____
_____

7. What rituals do you currently practice in your marriage or relationship?

_____
_____
_____
_____
_____

_____
_____
_____
_____
_____
_____
_____
_____
_____
_____
_____
_____
_____
_____
_____
_____
_____
_____
_____
_____
_____
_____
_____

8. What would you like to take away from this workbook?

_____
_____
_____
_____
_____
_____
_____
_____
_____
_____
_____

Working Marriages

S	R	E	S	P	E	C	T	P	T	S	U	R	T
L	O	Y	A	L	T	Y	G	A	T	U	U	A	C
D	T	Y	C	T	I	F	N	D	T	N	N	P	O
I	P	T	L	P	S	R	I	V	T	I	D	P	M
T	P	I	E	E	U	I	N	E	N	T	E	R	M
E	L	L	M	P	P	E	E	N	E	Y	R	E	U
T	O	A	P	A	P	N	T	T	M	C	S	C	N
E	V	U	A	T	O	D	S	U	T	A	T	I	I
A	E	Q	T	I	R	S	I	R	I	M	A	A	C
M	K	E	H	E	T	H	L	E	M	I	N	T	A
W	I	L	Y	N	A	I	C	E	M	T	D	I	T
O	D	A	P	C	I	P	O	S	O	I	I	O	I
R	S	Y	N	E	L	H	H	R	C	N	N	N	O
K	U	I	N	X	E	S	P	C	R	I	G	S	N

COMMITMENT
UNDERSTANDING
RESPECT
SUPPORT
LOVE
EQUALITY
LISTENING
EMPATHY
ADVENTURE
FRIENDSHIP
TEAMWORK
SEX
APPRECIATION
COMMUNICATION
PATIENCE
INITIMACY
LOYALTY
TRUST
KIDS
UNITY

Made in the USA
Las Vegas, NV
09 October 2024

96557666R00059